KS1 English Reading
Comprehension

This fabulous CGP Targeted Question Book is an ideal introduction to Comprehension for pupils who are new readers...

There's a huge variety of colourful activities, texts and engaging questions covering all the important skills. Plus, you'll find answers to everything at the back.

It doesn't stop there! You'll find self-assessment boxes on each page and a table for recording tricky words to help track progress. Amazing!

What CGP is all about

Our sole aim here at CGP is to produce the highest quality books — carefully written, immaculately presented and dangerously close to being funny.

Then we work our socks off to get them out to you — at the cheapest possible prices.

Contents

Playtime	1
At the beach	2
Yes or no?	3
Colour the picture	4
In my pencil case	5
Can you finish it?	6
Finish the group	7
A pirate adventure!	8
What is the order?	9
Who said what?	10
Little Miss Muffet	11
Finish the sentences	12
Omar's diary	13
Match the sentence	14
Spot the odd one out	15
Which animal is it?	16

What are you eating?	18
In the park	20
Reasons	22
Party time	23
At the airport	24
The giant panda	26
What is the question?	27
A postcard to Gran	28
A surprise for Mum	29
Jack and the Beanstalk	30

Answers	31
Tricky words	34

Published by CGP

Editors: Siân Butler, Gabrielle Richardson, Kirsty Sweetman

With thanks to Eleanor Claringbold and Gareth Mitchell for the proofreading.
With thanks to Emily Smith for the copyright research.

Cover and Images throughout the book © www.edu-clips.com

ISBN: 978 1 78294 758 5
Printed by Elanders Ltd, Newcastle upon Tyne.

Text, design, layout and original illustrations
© Coordination Group Publications Ltd. (CGP) 2022
All rights reserved.

Photocopying this book is not permitted, even if you have a CLA licence.
Extra copies are available from CGP with next day delivery • 0800 1712 712 • www.cgpbooks.co.uk

Playtime

Look at this picture of a park. Trace the letters.
Circle the four things that do not belong.

the park

> **Now try this**
>
> Colour in all the things that belong in the park.

Year 1 — Targeted Comprehension

At the beach

Trace over each word.
Colour in the things you would see at the beach.

sheep

sun hat

bucket

spade

milk

flip flops

crab

Now try this

Draw **three** more things you would see at the beach.

Year 1 — Targeted Comprehension

Yes or no?

Trace either '**yes**' or '**no**' to show if the sentence matches the picture or not.

yes

no

Laura dressed up as a princess.

yes

no

Barry has hurt himself.

yes

no

Clara wears glasses.

yes

no

Luke is a doctor.

Year 1 — Targeted Comprehension

Colour the picture

Read the text and circle each colour.

Colour the picture so it matches the text.

> The children are riding on a red bus. The driver has a blue hat. The bell is yellow. The flowers are pink.

Year 1 — Targeted Comprehension

In my pencil case

Count how many items there are in each group. Write the number in each sentence. The first one has been done for you.

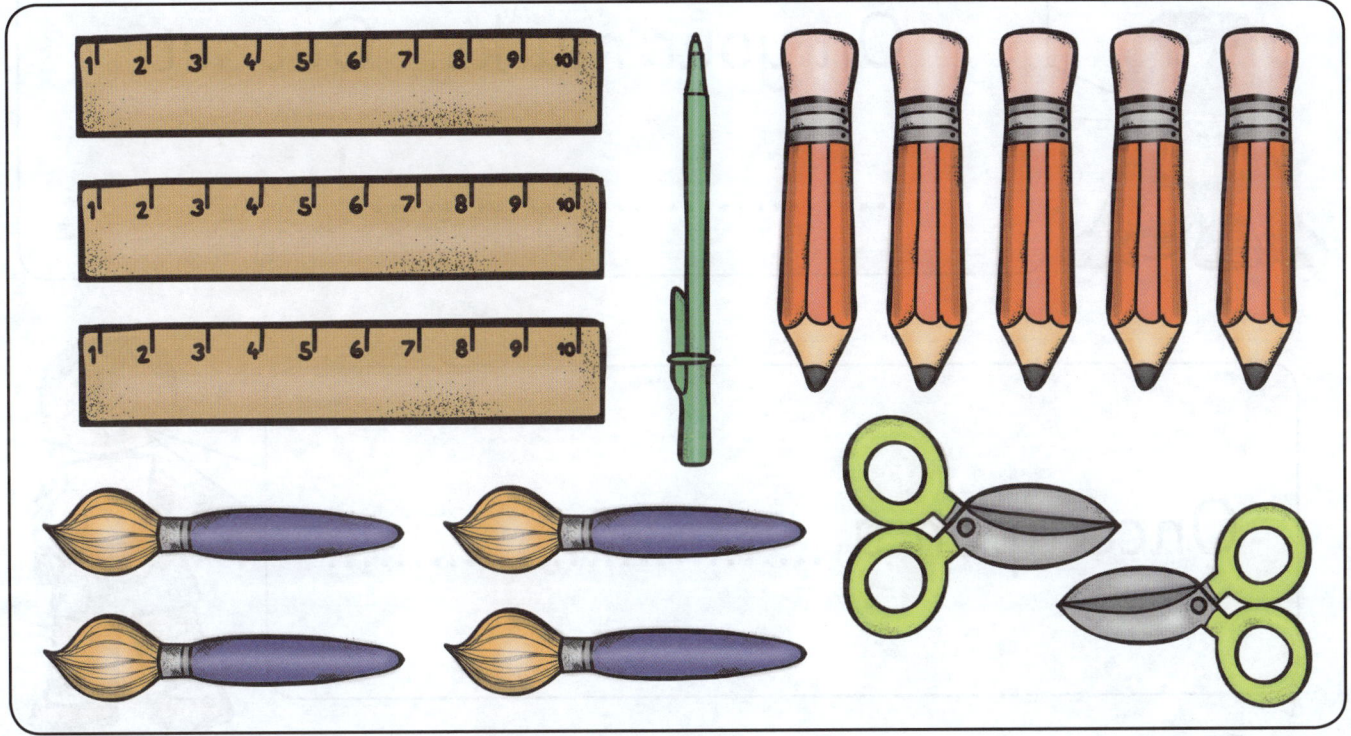

1. There are ....three........ rulers.

2. There are .... pencils.

3. There are .... paint brushes.

4. There are .... pairs of scissors.

Now try this

Write a sentence about something else you see in the picture.

Year 1 — Targeted Comprehension

Can you finish it?

Finish each speech bubble with the right word.

On your marks. Get set. ....!

Once upon a ....

They lived happily ever ....

Heads, shoulders, knees and ....

Finish the group

Trace over each word. Write a word that fits in each group. Then draw a picture of it.

fruit

....

animals

  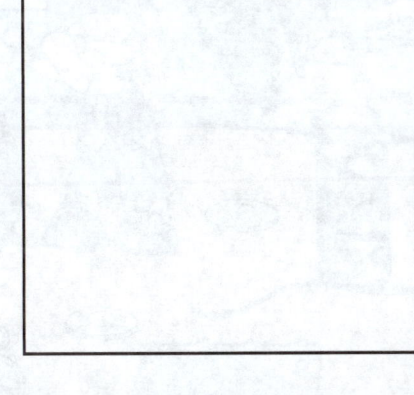

....

party

....

Year 1 — Targeted Comprehension

A pirate adventure!

Look at the picture. Find and circle these things.

① Two pirate flags

② A telescope

③ A pirate with an eye patch

④ Two different animals

Write the correct word from the box in the sentences.

| Josh   monkey   Josef   parrot |

.... is holding a sword.

There is a .... sitting on a treasure chest.

Year 1 — Targeted Comprehension

What is the order?

Look at the pictures. Put the words in the right order.
The first one has been done for you.

- [1] snow
- [3] melt
- [2] make

- [ ] chop
- [ ] peel
- [ ] dig

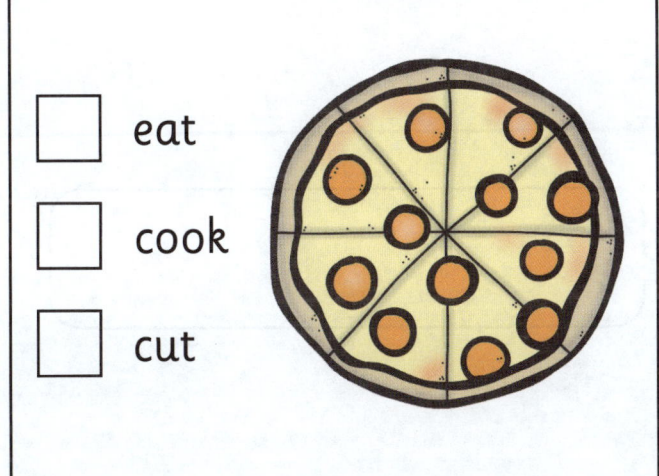

- [ ] eat
- [ ] cook
- [ ] cut

- [ ] toast
- [ ] eat
- [ ] spread

Now try this

Write your own three words in order about making breakfast.

Year 1 — Targeted Comprehension

Who said what?

Trace over each sentence. Draw lines to match each speech bubble to the right person.

I love sport!

It's my birthday.

I live in a castle.

I have a pet.

Now try this

Write a sentence about yourself, using these sentences to help.

Year 1 — Targeted Comprehension

Little Miss Muffet

Little Miss Muffet
Sat on a tuffet,
Eating her curds and whey;
Along came a spider
Who sat down beside her
And frightened Miss Muffet away.

Circle the action that Little Miss Muffet does **not** do.

      sits   sings   eats

Draw the last picture to match the story.

  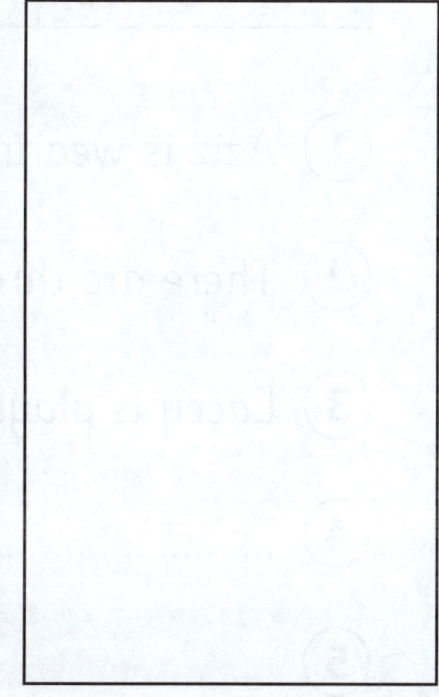

Year 1 — Targeted Comprehension

Finish the sentences

Look at the picture. Fill in the missing words.

1) Aziz is wearing a stripy ....

2) There are three green ....

3) Lacey is playing with two ....

4) .... has a pet snake.

5) .... is wearing an orange jumper.

Year 1 — Targeted Comprehension

Omar's diary

Read the diary entry. Colour in the animals that Omar saw.

> Dear Diary,
> I went to the farm with my sister. We saw a cow with spots and two pigs. There was a big duck in the pond. I like goats, but I didn't see any at the farm.

Now try this

Draw **two** more farm animals. Write down what they are.

Year 1 — Targeted Comprehension

Match the sentence

Look at the pictures. Tick the box next to the sentence that best describes each picture.

☐ Jose is afraid of insects.

☐ Jose loves insects.

"They are the best animals!"

Ace likes baking cakes. ☐

Ace hates baking cakes. ☐

"This is so much fun!"

"My knee hurts."

☐ Jessica needs a plaster.

☐ Jessica has lost her dog.

The ducks aren't hungry. ☐

The ducks are hungry. ☐

"Feed us!"

Now try this

Write the names of **two** insects that are near Jose.

Year 1 — Targeted Comprehension

Spot the odd one out

Circle the **two** sentences that match each picture.

Emma fed the chickens.

Anya played the flute.

Kamal listened to music.

Poppy has a cold.

Aditi flew a kite.

Farid has earache.

Mum goes to the shops.

Anna owns a pony.

Toby hugs his fish.

Which animal is it?

Trace over each word.

Draw lines to match each animal to its home.

dog

pig

robin

ladybird

nest

pen

leaves

kennel

Year 1 — Targeted Comprehension

Draw lines to match each speech bubble to the correct pet.

My pet hops around.

tortoise

My pet has a shell on her back.

fish

My pet lives in water.

parrot

My pet can fly.

rabbit

Now try this

Draw **two** more animals that people keep as pets.

Year 1 — Targeted Comprehension

What are you eating?

Put these pictures in the right order to tell a story.
Write **1**, **2**, **3** or **4** in the box to show the order.

Write the correct food from the box under each picture.

> peas egg bread
> cake banana lemon

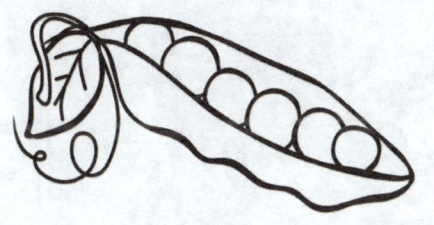 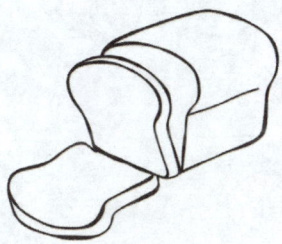

....

....

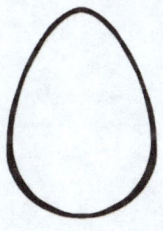 

....

Now try this

Colour in all the pictures of food that are **not** fruit.

Year 1 — Targeted Comprehension

In the park

Look at the picture. Who is...

① fishing? ....

② painting? ....

③ riding a bike? ....

④ playing chase? ....

⑤ taking a photo? ....

Year 1 — Targeted Comprehension

Look at the signs and read the sentences.
Tick the sentence that matches each sign.

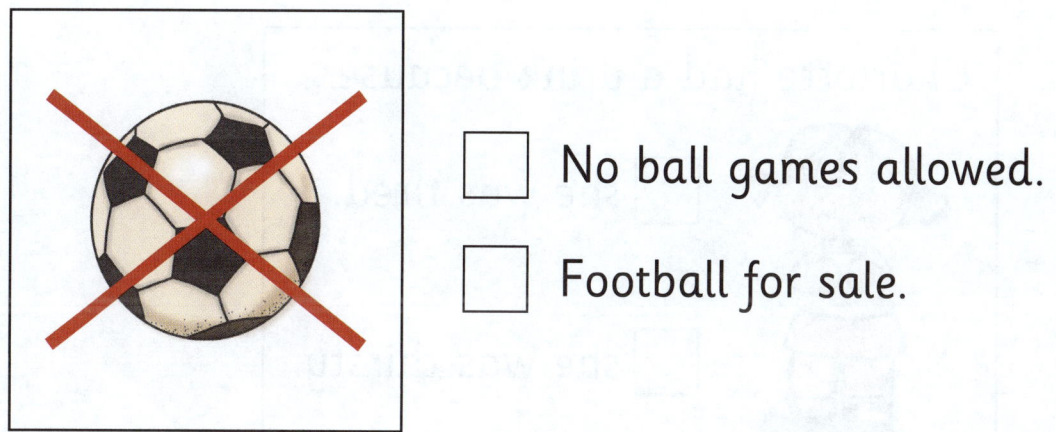

☐ No ball games allowed.

☐ Football for sale.

The cat is lost. ☐

The cat has won a prize. ☐

☐ We sell bus tickets.

☐ We sell boat tickets.

Now try this

Make a sign about a school rule for the wall in your classroom.

Year 1 — Targeted Comprehension

Reasons

Look at the pictures. Tick the box next to the reason why.

Charlotte had a drink because...
- ☐ she was tired.
- ☐ she was thirsty.

Luke washed his hands because... 
- ☐ he was about to eat.
- ☐ he had just taken a bath.

Gloria bought a present because... 
- ☐ it was her dad's birthday.
- ☐ it was raining.

Joel mopped the floor because...
- ☐ he was bored.
- ☐ it was dirty.

Now try this

Write down one more reason why Gloria might buy a present.

Year 1 — Targeted Comprehension

Party time

Read the letter. Answer the questions below.

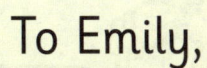

To Emily,

Please come to my 7th birthday party at my house on 12th May. It will start at 2 pm. It is a kings and queens party, so please dress up. I hope you can come!

Hadiza

(1) How old will Hadiza be on her birthday?

....

(2) Is the party in the morning or the afternoon?

....

(3) Colour in the outfit that Emily could wear to the party.

At the airport

Ruby

Claire

Langa

Leo

Daniel

Kiana

Put a tick next to all the sentences that are true.

☐   Three people have suitcases.
☐   Ruby has a camera.
☐   Daniel has some tickets.
☐   Claire is holding a passport.

Answer these questions in **full sentences**.

① How many people are there?

....

② Who has a sun on their T-shirt?

....

③ Who is wearing a hat?

....

④ Who is reading a map?

....

Now try this

Write a sentence to describe what Langa is wearing.

Year 1 — Targeted Comprehension

The giant panda

Most giant pandas live in China's forests.

They need to eat lots of a plant called bamboo to survive. At times, they also eat small animals and fish.

Eating enough bamboo is very important for pandas. They spend 10-16 hours feeding on it each day. The rest of their day is spent sleeping or relaxing.

1) Where do giant pandas live?

....

2) Colour in **two** pictures of foods that pandas eat.

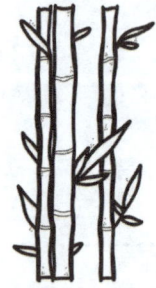 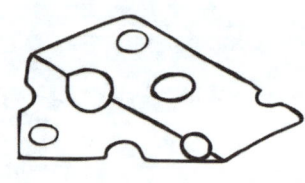 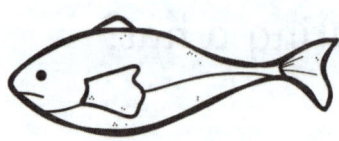 

3) What do pandas do for 10-16 hours each day?

....

Now try this

Draw **two** foods you like. Write down what they are called.

Year 1 — Targeted Comprehension

What is the question?

Read the answers. Write the questions in the speech bubbles.

....

....

My name is Rosie.

....

....

I am ten years old.

....

....

My favourite food is pizza.

Now try this

Write your own answers to the questions.

Year 1 — Targeted Comprehension

A postcard to Gran

Dear Gran,
I am having a great holiday!
Yesterday, we went to the beach.
Today, we are going on a boat.
I hope Max is okay and you are feeding him and taking him for walks.
See you soon.
Love, Jess

Gran
Daffodil Street
Manchester
England

1) Where did Jess go yesterday?

....

2) What is she doing today?

....

3) Who do you think Max is?

....

4) Find and **copy** a word from the postcard which shows Jess is enjoying her holiday.

....

A surprise for Mum

Read this story and answer the questions below.

Grandad was looking after Anita while Mum was at work. Grandad and Anita wanted to do something nice for Mum because she had been working hard. They baked a cake for Mum as a surprise. They also tidied the house and washed the car.

1) Which word best describes Anita and Grandad?

☐ mean   ☐ kind   ☐ silly

2) How do you think Mum felt when she came home?

☐ angry   ☐ sad   ☐ pleased

3) Give a reason for your choice in Question 2.

....

....

Now try this

Think of **two** more words to describe Anita and Grandad.

Year 1 — Targeted Comprehension

Jack and the Beanstalk

Once upon a time, there was a boy called Jack. Jack and his mother were very poor. All they owned was a cow. One day, Jack's mother sent him to the market to sell the cow. On the way to the market, Jack met an old man. The man didn't have any money. Instead, he gave Jack three beans for the cow. He told Jack they were magic beans. Jack went home with the beans. His mother was very angry. She threw the beans out of the window and sent Jack to bed.

1) Where did Jack meet the old man?

  ☐ outside his house   ☐ on the way to the market   ☐ at the market

2) Why do you think Jack's mother was angry?

....

....

3) What do you think happens next in the story?

....

....

Now try this

Draw **three** pictures that show what you wrote in question 3.

Year 1 — Targeted Comprehension

Answers

Page 1 — Playtime

You should have circled:

Page 2 — At the beach

You should have coloured:

Page 3 — Yes or no?

Laura dressed up as a princess. — **no**
Barry has hurt himself. — **yes**
Clara wears glasses. — **yes**
Luke is a doctor. — **no**

Page 4 — Colour the picture

You should have circled: red, blue, yellow, pink

Page 5 — In my pencil case

2. There are **five** pencils.
3. There are **four** paint brushes.
4. There are **two** pairs of scissors.

Page 6 — Can you finish it?

On your marks. Get set. **Go**!
Once upon a **time**
They lived happily ever **after**.
Heads, shoulders, knees and **toes**.

Page 7 — Finish the group

Any sensible answers, e.g.

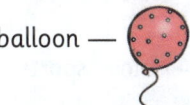

Page 8 — A pirate adventure!

You should have circled:

Josh is holding a sword.
There is a **monkey** sitting on a treasure chest.

Answers

Page 9 — What is the order?

3 chop
2 peel
1 dig

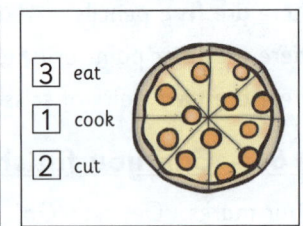
3 eat
1 cook
2 cut

1 toast
3 eat
2 spread

Page 10 — Who said what?

 — I have a pet.
 — I love sport!
 — It's my birthday.
 — I live in a castle.

Page 11 — Little Miss Muffet

You should have circled: sings
Any sensible picture, e.g.

Page 12 — Finish the sentences

1. Aziz is wearing a stripy **top** / **T-shirt**.
2. There are three green **frogs**.
3. Lacey is playing with two **rabbits**.
4. **Patrick** has a pet snake.
5. **Lucy** is wearing an orange jumper.

Page 13 — Omar's diary

You should have coloured:

Page 14 — Match the sentence

You should have ticked:
Jose loves insects.
Ace likes baking cakes.
Jessica needs a plaster.
The ducks are hungry.

Page 15 — Spot the odd one out

You should have circled:
Anya played the flute.
Kamal listened to music.
Poppy has a cold.
Farid has earache.
Anna owns a pony.
Toby hugs his fish.

Pages 16-17 — Which animal is it?

dog — kennel
pig — pen
robin — nest
ladybird — leaves

My pet hops around. —
My pet has a shell on her back. —
My pet lives in water. —
My pet can fly. —

Pages 18-19 — What are you eating?

 3
 4

Year 1 — Targeted Comprehension   Answers

Answers

You should have written:

— peas
— bread 
— lemon 
— cake 
— egg 
— banana 

Pages 20-21 — In the park

1. Maja
2. Robert
3. Alice
4. Sam and Jola
5. Hiro

You should have ticked:
No ball games allowed.
The cat is lost.
We sell bus tickets.

Page 22 — Reasons

You should have ticked:
she was thirsty.
he was about to eat.
it was her dad's birthday.
it was dirty.

Page 23 — Party time

1. seven
2. the afternoon
3. You should have coloured:

Pages 24-25 — At the airport

You should have ticked:
Three people have suitcases.
Daniel has some tickets.

1. There are six people.
2. Leo has a sun on his T-shirt.
3. Kiana is wearing a hat.
4. Ruby is reading a map.

Page 26 — The giant panda

1. in China's forests
2. You should have coloured:

3. feed on bamboo

Page 27 — What is the question?

What is your name?
How old are you?
What is your favourite food?

Page 28 — A postcard to Gran

1. the beach
2. going on a boat
3. her pet dog
4. great

Page 29 — A surprise for Mum

1. You should have ticked: kind
2. You should have ticked: pleased
3. Any sensible answer, e.g. Anita and Grandad did jobs to help her and they made a cake to eat.

Page 30 — Jack and the Beanstalk

1. You should have ticked: on the way to the market
2. Any sensible answer, e.g. They are poor and needed the money from the cow, but Jack swapped the cow for beans.
3. Any sensible answer, e.g. A beanstalk grows and Jack climbs it. Jack steals from the giant at the top then chops down the beanstalk.

Answers   Year 1 — Targeted Comprehension

Tricky words

Write down any tricky words from the book here.
Tick them once you know what they mean.

Tricky word	✓

Tricky word	✓